Black Holes
and
Their Feeding Habits

Black Holes
and
Their Feeding Habits

Kiyoko Reidy

Terrapin Books

© 2025 by Kiyoko Reidy
Printed in the United States of America.
All rights reserved.
No part of this book may be reproduced in any manner, except for brief quotations embodied in critical articles or reviews.

Terrapin Books
4 Midvale Avenue
West Caldwell, NJ 07006

www.terrapinbooks.com

ISBN: 978-1-947896-81-9
Library of Congress Control Number: 2025932303

First Edition

Cover art by Hannah Blackwell
Little One, Mixed Media, 5.5" x 8.5"
2017

for Kame and my Obaasan

Contents

Black Holes and Their Feeding Habits   3

I
My Little Brother Tells Me He's a Drug Addict   7
On the birthday in which I am
    having relationship problems   9
Francis Bacon on *The Black Triptychs*   10
Business Ethics   13
Self-Portrait as Minotaur   15
I run outside when I hear her   17
Portrait of My Brother with His Habit   19
Cocke County   21

II
Haibun for the Language My Obaasan Still Remembers   25
On My Way to Being an Actual   27
Francis Bacon on *Three Studies for Figures*
    at the Base of a Crucifixion   29
All the Men in My Life Are Sick   32
Listening to Coltrane While Watching
    You Play Video Games   34
In the Time of Home Improvement Projects   36
What Will Live   38
My Mother as Cicada   40
At the Center for Imaging   43

III

Only Air	47
Fishing	49
Driving Past the Fortune Teller	51
Letter to an Ex-Lover	52
The Good Stuff	54
Invitation	55
Jesus in the Foothills	56
At the Cemetery	58
Obed Wild and Scenic River	59
Entering the Anza Borrego	61
My Brother as Anonymous Bather	62

IV

Self-Portrait with Francis in My Ear	67
Oregon with Wildfire	68
At Sun Rock Ranch	70
My Obaasan Once Made a Skirt of Cranes	71
The Record	73
In Which I Can Forgive My Obaasan	75
In Which I Cannot	76
Origin	77
I watch basketball with B and yell	79
Relapse with Memory of the Ramsey Cascades	80
Apologia	82

Emergence	85

Acknowledgments	89
About the Author	91

Black Holes and Their Feeding Habits

*—after polarized photos of the black hole
at the center of the M87 galaxy*

When black holes pull in other bodies—space junk, small planets, products of evolution—it's called feeding. Impossible vortex of gravity made human, made hungry. I learn this on the Cumberland Plateau in a house rented for the weekend. Wood walls are pocked with bullet holes and the river is so low it's become something else. Mud wash. Silt thick. I push a stick three feet into the riverbed and it keeps sinking. I want to step off the bank into muck—ankle deep, knees, hips. When something is sucked into the black hole, it compresses horizontally and elongates vertically—the process is called *spaghettification*. If the most powerful forces we know can't maintain some dignity, what chance is there for the rest of us? I avoid tools that possess devastating power: telescopes, guns. I've never even held a gun—I came closest at a party, a friend's house tucked into the hazy base of the Appalachians. Two men found a rifle in a closet after hours of drinking themselves loose. In the kitchen they played at battle, miming the kick back, the body's caves—a clean kill. I couldn't look away. The gun's dark eye swiveled around the room, settling at my chest. The abyss stared back. I was told if there's a gun in a poem, it needs to go off. *Bang,* one man said. *Bang, bang.* The point at which nothing can escape the gravitational force of the black hole is called the event horizon. Past the horizon, nothing returns—light, matter, knowledge. The black eye spun away. I watched until the gun was abandoned, the men bored with the muzzle in their mouths, the adrenaline high fizzling out like a bad firework. What happens when tragedy passes us by? Their bodies twisted beneath the kitchen's single bulb, the pull of each man warping the light toward his mouth, imagined bullet tunneling the skull. The house where I stood with the rifle's *o* pressed into my sternum burned years later in a total loss fire. Except, freed from the wood by flame, they found bullets in the ruins. On earth, something is always there, blanketed in ash. The newest images, polarized, taken with a global web of telescopes, reveal the swirl of the electromagnetic field, a sun in inverse: red and yellow spiraling into the singularity—uncertain bullseye, slack mouth of oblivion.

I

My Little Brother Tells Me He's a Drug Addict

At Christmas time, our parents' house ablaze
with light, glimmery trinkets, the thick
smell of cut firs. The low wail of a holiday chorus

slips under the door. It could be a funeral
song, but instead *all is calm, all is bright*.
We talk in his childhood bedroom, knee to knee

on the red metal bunk we used to share.
Hesitant in our affection, as though meeting
after years of another life, I try to see

what's stayed the same: his huge mess of hair like
hydrangea blooms, pupils wide and dark
as wild blueberries. I want to touch his cheek,

to know this stranger who moves
my brother's body in and out of reality.
He won't name names, leaves me

to imagine what all he has welcomed
into himself. Maybe a better sister
would have known, trusted the urges

to check the crooks of his elbows
for little graves, called five times
instead of four when he missed

our weekly coffee date. Instead, I let
missed meetings pile up between us, left
terse voicemails and felt sorry to have a brother

who could not love me how I wanted. Now,
it's the season of giving and I am willing to give
anything. I just want a brother

who lives. Tinsel rustles on the door frame.
It's dinner time. We sit side by side
at the big table like children, our white plates

staring back at us.

On the birthday in which I am having relationship problems,

my father orders me an orchid—pink
blooms and stalks with heads heavy as soldiers
after battle. On the phone, he says, *Happy
quarter century. If you take care of it,
it will last a long time.* In the sandy dirt
is an instruction card: ounces of water
per week, desired temperature, humidity.
It is the worst kind of gift—one that becomes, almost
instantly, a responsibility. I want what's beautiful

to stay beautiful. Sure—I'm selfish. I'm threatened
by other things that need. Still, I love
my father. I try for weeks: five ounces of water
on Fridays, sun-striped shelf by the window, wet air
that leaves me sweaty when I sleep.

                                 My most tender
care makes no difference—the stem's sickly
yellowing, waking to find another bloom
dead overnight. At least I will be able to reuse
the ceramic pot—to hold, next time, a pile of shells
or a cactus. When my father visits, he won't question
what's no longer here.

Francis Bacon on *The Black Triptychs*

I

In threes all good things both come and die—drinks,
luck, lovers. George, you were the third love to leave
that year, and like any year the worst is saved
for last. You died while I greeted guests and dignitaries
at the Grand Palais. I smiled as you turned
to flesh alone. Someone else discovered you, but
I see you still—skin mottled as a plum,
ruined features—heaped nose, drooping chin—

undeniably yours. The light fills your hollows
like poison, shadow spills across the hotel
floor: silhouette of wings, black lungs. My mind
is a gallery of your face moving through
its easy drunkenness, your cheeks soft with liquor.
Now with three long fingers raised, Death follows me.

II

With three fingers raised, Death follows me now—
I can paint nothing but you, George, face ravaged
by want, black wrapping your chest like a bandage
and I don't know if Death is counting up or down.
Milky light and the pills, your final sacrament,
fill up your body as you once filled mine.
Mottled pink flesh, coiled wet as intestine—
I wonder if you, vacillant love, could truly intend this.

My mind, once able to devise anything,
now curves only toward you, compels me
to some uncertain note, your face my tuning fork.
I swathe my lips in paint and the canvas sings
your death hymn. Architect of revelry, artist
of my heart, *all colors will agree in the dark.*

III

Like the ready dark, all colors agree
in my chest, night breaks and the dawn spills open
like a mouth. It has been years, but I've chosen
you again, in profile, with all the injuries
I've wrung in—your throat a spring, a mirror,
then a chord of hands. These days I paint mostly
myself, your voice as a vein of white, ghostly
trick of shadow. Dead men in my sheets, devourers

of my art—you are the only haunt who guides
my tongue to water and my hand to the brush
when the heart's black milk nearly drives me blind.
Still, I drink and screw and all the while have denied
this portrait will be my last. My mind in its dusk—
can you tell, George? Is it your face or mine?

Business Ethics

In the hottest months we hunted
>and traded their bodies: cicada's alien husks

still clinging to the dogwoods,
>monarch wings resplendent as church windows,

the dead June bug's
>lustrous exoskeleton alive with light.

Neighborhood kids
>dull with the long suburban summer,

we became sharp-eyed
>collectors, resilient hagglers. These fragile

remnants were our currency.
>We were proud and greedy, the allure of business

already softening our principles.
>White linens and gift boxes, table runners

and doilies—we stole
>from our parents, dreaming of the finest backdrops

for our driveway displays,
>our precious dead arranged carefully atop

mother's best napkins.
>We shooed away the younger kids, afraid

their uncertain steps
>would crush our inventory, or they would pocket

some good find, eager consumers
>oblivious to the workings of our modest economy.

We wined and dined
>each other with cold glasses of lemonade

as we scurried between
>our miniature storefronts, our dealings covetous

and uncompromising.
     A younger boy, in search of his own profits, once tried to join our market—
     he brought a jar of fireflies collected the night before, now heaped like a small pile
     of black beans against the glass floor. When he shook the jar, trying to coax them
     out of death, they rattled like a sad maraca. None of us were fooled.
     He was too young to understand the transgressions that are permissible
     in the pursuit of fortune, and those that are not.

Self-Portrait as Minotaur

Years between these long
                thin rooms. Life
of corridors, doorway
                to a doorway. Along one wall: onions line
                a shelf, white bulbs
bright as bone in the cool
                dark. Potatoes

heaped like golden
                fists. Beneath the jaw's
cusp: no rhythm. Denied
                even the body's
metronome. Here,
                nothing rots:
root home, wine
                keep. Always the bitter

edge of arrival, the mind's
                talent for suspension.
From above: whorl of these
                walls, print of God's
own massive finger, swirl
                of his eye—and its center: me,
the pupil, black chasm,
                lightless hallway.

This stagnancy: its own kind
    of decay. I am the tunnel
into the mountain. I am more
    beast every day.

I run outside when I hear her

scream, the sound ripping
from our neighbor's quiet okusan
followed by the silence of knowing
she's lost nearly everything.
her husband at her feet,
draped on the stairs of their home like a
drying towel. He is drunk
or, was. The sweet sharp of awamori
hot in his throat. The snake, gold
diamond-backed Okinawan
habu, is still attached, fangs sunk like
stakes deep in the flesh
of his calf. The snake, too, is dead.
There is no winner here. He must
have walked home
through unlucky jungle or sugar
cane when he was bit,
too drunk and scared to think of anything
but running away. You can't run
from what is already in you.
I wonder know if this is what sister,
seven and gone
from snakebite, looked like:
purple-lipped and still,

scream, the thin wail of fear
followed by the victory of animal
over animal. My obaasan
stands beneath our southern
magnolia tree, full with velvet
blossoms big as a face,
her eyes wet and wild, a hoe wrapped
in her arthritic hands. At her feet:
a black rat snake cut to pieces
in the glossy leaves. Rat snakes
are no danger to anything
human, eat only rodents small
Enough to swallow. Her ankles
spattered with dirt or blood.
she is as still as the snake which
is to say completely. This is the first
time I am scared of her, this woman
who loves me to sleep, who teaches
me to count in Okinawan and fills
the counters with squares of mochi.
The first time I am glad the tools
stay outside at night. This is a fresh,
soft horror: scales and layered
flesh, thin tongue lolling. I bend

body laying a little wrong.		to touch the snake's lonely head
The backyard is full of		and my obaasan snaps in a mother's
sisters, one brother,			voice, gone the softness of age.
Driftwood to mark each small		from below, she is towering. White
grave, rising from the earth like	petals and cut snake at her feet like
				some sort of garden.

Portrait of My Brother with His Habit

Though the internet claims
it takes twenty-one days
to form a new habit, I am here
to tell you it only takes a single
moment of choice, then a lifetime
to un-make—powder
falling up through a slip
of sunlight into his nose or a loose
handful of pills, dead white
bugs in his palm; without sense
of where his body began or how
it could end, he bent
the world to his will:
he traced his wants onto air
and they solidified, he drew windows
on his arms and filled them with stars,
black holes the size of a needle's
point, tiny mouths with
their unremitting hungers, and all
the while I went on assuming
the worst, though what I imagined
was the worst was not, and even
once he told me I couldn't really
imagine—a body of doors swinging
loosely on their hinges, the twenty-one
days coming and coming again, an army
of days that were all the day
he was going to quit, the day he'd

rewind, walking backward
through every opening he'd made until
he stood at the entrance
to himself, the first door
of this life I couldn't imagine,
and finally he'd slam it shut,
all the other doors behind it
falling like dominoes.

Cocke County

The men ring their birds, uncertain
orbit of battle, backup dancers
to their roosters. What feathers
not already plucked, now stained
the pale dirt, crimson confetti
at the long party's end.
      The men needed something
to quicken their blood, something
to think of in bed beside
their tired wives. The birds' red
ridge of flesh. Carnage
of wing and cockspur. Hats tipped
low over their eyes to disguise it:
the wild lusting for a violence
different than the dull brutality of living.
      They busted the cockfighting pit
less than an hour from my home
when I was nine. When the FBI raided,
nobody would claim the three hundred
gamecocks present at the pit—arced gaffs
roped to their ankles, wattles severed
to prevent the opponent's advantage. The news
said nothing about the manner of execution. When
the people arrested in the raid claimed cockfighting
was part of what kept their communities alive, I was
unforgiving. I was a child and quick to condemn
cruelty. This morning, researching the cockfights
and the raid on Appalachia's largest

and oldest fighting pit, an ad popped up with a video
of two roosters locked in fatal step, their men sulking
behind them like oversized shadows.
        I watched. I watched
the terminal dance, the birds' breasts unzipping
in the low, pixelated light, the throbbing
of wings, the feathers gleaming on the red clay like slivers
of moon. I had wagered nothing on this fight;
knew nothing of blood sport. It didn't matter.
I watched because I had to watch, because I felt
the rush too close to pleasure that comes
from knowing something is fighting
for its life, and this time, mercifully, it's not you.

II

Haibun for the Language My Obaasan Still Remembers

Two Okinawan sisters in muumuus at a card table on the big island. Half glasses of bad wine and talk of Kumejima: spiral shells—as big as a baby—that ani pulled from the ocean floor, sake drunk father too unsteady to walk the cliffs home alone. They use the names of those both loved and dead sparingly. Still the same nightmares: well fed snakes round as papayas, knots of leather and bark tucked in a child's cheek, the sheer drop to meet the ocean. Too little time to visit all the mind's graves. Tipsy from drink and the pleasure of togetherness again, nearly two decades gone, they laugh at the new world's bizarreries: Dr. Oz listing beni-imo, the small purple potato of Okinawa, as one of the year's best superfoods. My obaasan tells Sumiko about finding beni-imo mounded in cardboard bins at the Walmart in Junction City, Kansas, where she has lived for the last fifty years. Her utter disbelief. *They must have sprouted arms and swum across the ocean. How else would they get to America? Potatoes that can swim! A real super food.* They break into laughter, shielding their mouths with their hands, embarrassed at the looseness of their joy. My obaasan speaks in spliced sentences—sworn off her childhood tongue for most of a life, sometimes she digs through a vocabulary too small in both languages and comes up empty. Her fingers rummage through the air, find nothing but the hills and grooves of Sumiko's palms. The memory of

                ripe mango passes
            over the mind's landscape
                 like a summer rain.

On My Way to Being an Actual

Perhaps it will happen
when, if ever, I purchase
some square of earth. Or
publish a book. Grow
a child. Cook lamb
for a dinner party. Be recognized
at the grocery store. Or
when, like my parents
before me, I buy
a decorative vase
to display on a shelf only
ever used for what is delicate
and rich. Perhaps then. Yes,
surely then. I am lost
in the bounty of this life. As a child
I thought often of death
from drinking too much water—
strange fact I plucked
from the internet. What we know
we learn somehow. The heart
can drown. There is too much
of a good thing and so much
of everything. I hear the people
are buying couch cushion covers
for their covered couch cushions.
So I do, too. How else to treat
something precious? Braised lamb,
my guests and children moving through

these crowded rooms. Perhaps
now. Yes, surely now—and still
the veined and beating muscle sinking,
sinking like a fist and still my mouth
pressed to the running tap—gulping
wildly, marveling at all this abundance.

Francis Bacon on *Three Studies for Figures at the Base of a Crucifixion*

    I.

I only wanted to breathe, Father. To open
my asthmatic lungs to sky. A throat packed
with light. I know, I failed how you taught me to act.
Unable to mount a horse without choking
and the hounds' cold baying made a poor lullaby.
But the mind learns to play when the body
cannot. The claustrophobic rooms made me.
These devils of flesh come now to rectify

my childhood in the wet dark—their heads, all gaped
mouth, bulbous body, neck warped as a dead swan,
muted howl climbing the spine, damp rings of teeth.
They gnash at my heels. I cannot escape
your voice: *Asthma is a weak heart, no brawn.*
Speak up, son. Father, if I had breath, I would have screamed.

II.

Each breath of the hounds ending in a wail—
in my dreams I am the frightened animal
pursued by you, Father, with your damnable
pride and muscled horse. Your coat's crimson tails,
a clear warning: *nothing will survive me*.
Your lesson—love between men grows as tempered
violence. To love otherwise is to surrender
everything. Look. I have brought my beastly

wants into form. On the left, I desire
a man for the first time—you. I cannot
suffer to show that face. They are allowed
no sight, no smell. Father, red-clad rider,
you'd track your hounds into any black heart.
I know this lust. These are the beasts I follow.

III.

These beasts, my wrung trinity of lust—
you cannot help but hate what is human
in them: white rag around the neck, blooming
of the ear. Perhaps you think your disgust
rendered me unable to find the locus
of my joy. Perhaps it would do your darkness
good to believe it was you who tarnished
this mind. No. I painted Christ's body, broken

by all our salacious appetites; then his face
bracing the sky. I destroyed every nerve
of oil and wood—that, like me, wasn't meant to survive.
Each canvas scrubbed white, each portrait erased.
Again and again I gave you a glory you didn't deserve.
It was you, Father, exalted and crucified.

All the Men in My Life Are Sick

All the men in my life are sick:
        bodies expanding where

they should not, mind turning over
        like a gutted engine, vertebrae tight

and grinding. The women of my family care
        for their lovers how they can, spend whole

summers bent at the waist making things
        grow—winding weeds around their fingers

and yanking, weaving tomato vines
        through wide metal nets. It is a skill

that missed me. I fear killing even
        the cactus, fleshy pads leaving

invisible stingers in my hands. The fear
        fulfills itself, my panicked overcare

seeding chaos in my mother's garden.
        The morning glories close like fists.

My mother's arms sun-soft, a peach gone
        too ripe, skin pulling gently away

from the fruit. I walk through my parents'
        house, air bristling with spikey palms,

banana plants throwing broad shadows,
        and I catalog all the beautiful things

that require nothing from me. I claim
        them silently, wonder how I will keep

the objects that belong in this house
        when they are no longer here. My mother,

grandmother—they might live
        forever. but my father, brother, lover.

It will be important to learn the movements
        of grief. At night I'll hear the *tink* of metal

on metal, wonder if it's wind chimes
        or the ghost of his fingers fumbling

for an ice cream spoon.
        On the back patio, a bee hits the window

and falls like a sky stone into my coffee.
        I haunt this house that doesn't yet belong

to me, moving like a widow
        from window to window.

Listening to Coltrane While Watching You Play Video Games

year   of jazz
in darkness year of hands
cut   on something   I couldn't see
barely believed the blood
was mine   flesh
too thick in gauze and tape
my fist a tool   useless for loving
half your face shadowed blue, pupils
scuttle   back and forth
like trapped bugs   a saxophone
solo climbs over the sounds of war
          but you won't be outdone
yell at your diminished life
insincerity   of animated death   listen
for the reliable high hat's sharp shush
in the black   a small piece
of unshifting ground   it is easier to love
if we can't see what body
we're stuck with   though I do miss the strange ticks
of your mouth: lips folding   into petals
tongue skimming the cusp
of mustache your teeth   grinding like stones
under the low throb of bass   we buy plants
        together   knowing   they'll die
unceremoniously   philodendron
silk leafed and doomed   heart-leaves

like the soft   crunch of beetles
beneath bare feet   honest
and final   with their end
we discover   so many house plants
       are poisonous to our dogs
but it takes   precious time
to learn this

In the Time of Home Improvement Projects

This week they are repainting
my apartment building,
as though a fresh breath
of color was all it needed
to become worth living
in. Rarely does anything make
itself desirable all at once, though
that has never stopped anyone
from hoping. Section by section
the building puts on its best face—
like a child finally allowed
her mother's makeup. I asked my dog
what he thought of the sheet metal's
olive sheen, the coral highlights
bright enough to stun—
then remembered his color
blindness, his walls just shifting
from one shade of sickly green
to another.

Finally, the project reaches
my apartment: thick plastic pulled
taught over windows and sliding glass,
my small reminders of the world's
continuity now filmy and opaque.
The evening light filtered down
to almost nothing. I slip open

the balcony door, push
my fist into the thick cellophane.
When I pull back, the plastic
is stretched, wilted and finely
wrinkled: the skin at an old woman's
throat, delicate creases of silk.
Emboldened, I press my face
in next, neck straining against
the tension, and imagine my features'
ghostly emergence on the other side.
I cave my mouth, stretch my jaw
long and strange, eyes like empty
rooms, trying to be my most
terrifying. But it is late, and all
the painters have gone home.
There is no one left for me
to haunt.

What Will Live

—with a modified line from "the lost baby poem" by Lucille Clifton

They say a woman's body   releases its best
      eggs first   eleven years old
and my body already dark
      with possibility
first blood   not bright as a line
of petals but the color of damp earth   *what then did I know*
      of drowning,
of being drowned—

      now thirteen years
of twelve cycles   : that's one hundred and fifty-six
      of my best
work, finest craftmanship   taken up month
      after month
in the crimson squall the storm's unblinking
      eye   I
beg myself   stop   wait   keep what is good
      what will live—

lineage of miscarriage   mother, mother's mother
      pocked with graves   and my body still
mutely flushing   my best chance at a life
      the heart's uncertain   inheritance—

now, the hundred and fifty-seventh denial   wait
      wait
I bleed with abandon   as usual
      overnight

the animals take   to the trash bins, clawed hands
    unspooling my tissue
wrapped tampons   clotted brown
    hue of spoiled meat
strewn across the concrete, like missiles anticipating
    detonation
or wounds awaiting   a body.

My Mother as Cicada

I dream my mother a cicada: her flesh gone hard, wings pulling from her back, veins spreading translucent rainbow like oil over water. She rises as a false locust, thick-bodied and screaming, red eyes blank.

Her scream, or song, a series of ribs buckling: the tymbal, crashing in on itself and refilling, the empty chamber of her new body echoing like drums in a cave. The crash and refill so fast the clicking rises to a steady hum, loud enough to ruin a good ear.

In the dream, she crouches in the living room of my grandparents' house, spindly legs braced against the furniture, wings fluttering the overhead lights, stunted antennae waving blindly. The room is not how I remember it—but it's how I have seen it in pictures: my mother as a child, positioned seriously in a miniature rocking chair, bruised knees pulled tightly together, oversized glasses catching the light. One of the cicada's legs twitches against the same tiny chair. The sound of her singing slams around inside my sleep.

I have dreamed her this way for nearly eight years, huge bug hard-bodied and too loud, crammed into the shrunken parameters of my grandparents' house. Eight years ago was a new beginning in a cycle that has turned like a wheel for nearly two million years—a multiple of seventeen, a year of emergence.

Seventeen years of sucking at plant roots; nymphs pulling xylem, amber honey water, into their rounded bodies. Then, the seventeenth time spring's sweetness touched their mouths—a call to break ground and shed their hunched forms for a new hue: metal green and glistening. Eight years ago was a summer of millions: the trees thick with them, branches weighted, sagging.

Eight years ago was the summer my mom sat across from me in a restaurant booth, stared into her salad and cried, salting the limp lettuce. She told me how her father hurt her. He taught her daughters belonged to their fathers, fathers were entitled to what they wanted. She was taught to lay silent and halved and breathe slowly and after, to try to forget.

I left the restaurant with this new knowledge, the two of us the same mother and daughter but now different: our old skins left behind, expressions frozen, unmoving and brittle in the booth. The day's relentless heat made fuller still, chorused with cicada song.

For eight years I have dreamed her as cicada to give voice to her body, the sleeping mind's attempt to allow her sound, song, scream. The ribs caving, the echo's hollow pool. If she must bear this impossible weight, I want the collapse to be loud and haunting; I want to know her body will refill, will reclaim its shape.

A sun graced life of little more than two weeks, cicadas die unapologetically, bodies like bullets scattered haphazardly in the streets. Sometimes they pile at the base of trees, a heap of glimmer. But only after they have laid eggs: little pellets tucked in the grooves of branches, prepared to fall to the dirt, burrow, and wait. Their cycle, thirteen or seventeen years—always prime—designed to outwit predators with their patience, their meticulous understanding of time. I imagine them beneath me always: tunneling, pulling sweetness from woody roots, molting as they grow, flourishing in the earth's warm darkness.

At the Center for Imaging

Stinging nettle mashed or dried, dandelion
leaves with their bitter milk—steep in tea,
add to salad, or prayer. In the waiting room,

all the women are pregnant, and I am
jealous. One moth clings to a lit
bulb, its feet burning with light,

tiny brain firing off with pleasure.
The prefix *mis*—originally meant
to change; now: ill, wrong, absence,

negation. As though change flows only
downstream, the direction of loss. My mother
describes field dressing a deer in detail: winding

through thick cords of intestine
like combing a daughter's hair. The snow
dotted with birds, dark bodies against the white.

While my organs flash like abstract art
on the screen, someone leans into the sky at the apex
of the world's tallest building seventy-five

hundred miles away. Still, someone builds toward
heaven, as though they've learned
nothing. Still, we risk it—proliferation

of language, the collapse into confusion.
The technician with her mouth ajar
asking when I'll meet with the doctor.

The other nurse in the room looking
worried, or just exhausted. Only one man died
building the Burj Khalifa. If we had known

in advance, the building would have been
built anyway. To call something an attempt
is to admit failure. In front of me, the uterus. A dark bean

on the ultrasound, set in the body's center and cut
through by a crease of light—my vanishing point.

III

Only Air

Below me, my brother's body
        thrashes wildly in the pool
       thin limbs   lashing my arms and chest,
   I push his head down
      once   twice   again below the water

though never for more   than a second
                        or two
   then I let him break
                for breath, watch him sucking air
  as though he were drowning,
        really drowning—
the whites of his eyes streaked red
    with chlorine, strained from playing
              at death's soft boundary.

We loved   like that. Or at least I loved him
    like that: my larger body above him
        in the pool, my hands pushing
           him forward   then tugging quickly back
     from the cusp
          of some ruin I would never fully intend.
I made his youth   into a thin wire he learned to walk,
    then, to revel in the art   of balance.

Because I loved him like that, maybe that's how he loves
          himself now, most comfortable
           with nothing but air below him, performing
    his only trick: rush of wind

                        in his face, cocktail of pills churning
his stomach, as he toes that same unmarked boundary of death—
too far to coax him back to safety,
        I pray: once   twice   again
                                        he'll come out alive.

Fishing

He baited worm after worm, digging
them from a white Styrofoam cup,
as each cast came back empty, the drag of the water my only
hope. He sat on our fishless,
ice-filled cooler, relentlessly patient,
his eyes in the shadow of his baseball
cap. The trout pond guaranteed fish heaped
high, but I wanted the catfish with their whiskered faces
and yawning, gummy mouths—eyes
both wise and dull at once. My grandfather
wound the live worms onto the hook—
pierce and fold on repeat until its ends
dangled limply like a fleshy noodle
on the thin barb. He never touched
me, never guided my arms over
my shoulder to teach the perfect
cast. I was terrible—I hooked the back
of my shirt, the tall grass at the pond's
edge, the thick meat of his palm. His mouth
opened like a gash, but he didn't yell.
He pulled the hook from his hand
like a metal splinter. When I remember these trips
we are alone, the two of us at the water's edge.
But I know now we never were, alone,
fishing or anywhere—always my mom
or grandmother watching, just outside
memory's vision. I learned, at sixteen,
what he did to my mom. Every fish he opened

was her. Their gills flashed in the bloody dark.
The truth slips back into the water and you know it only
by its hook-scarred mouth. I do not forgive him
his evils. The pond is full of many truths:
he was my grandfather; he was the cause
of pain; once, I hated him; once,
I loved him; once, I was a child, it was my birthday,
and I didn't catch a single fish.

Driving Past the Fortune Teller

maybe we should get a reading,
      he says, staring at the flat, low roof,
the windows covered in open
      palms, dozens of high fives left hanging.
Peeling posters taped
      to cinderblock: *tarot, crystal ball, chiromancy.*
I veer hard toward the two-car lot—
      the yelp of the wheels surprising us both.
I guess I am running
      out of options. If it takes magic to show you,
fine. This desperation
      has no glamour, is no longer cinematic. Every angle
is tired. I had good luck gone
      on too long. I knock on the building's grimy door,
then on the window. Nothing;
      which is, I imagine, how it must be. The glass
shudders in its frame, my reflection trembling.
      You're still in the car, whining my name. My knuckles
rest in the palm of a window
      decal. At the palm's center: a dark eye. I unspool my fist,
blanket the stare. Look
      at my hands. Tell me what I already know.

Letter to an Ex-Lover

I miss the prairies most, the tall shoots
        of goldenrod; cattails in late winter—strange seeds
        still hoarding their soft fluff; the prairie
            blazingstar emerging as a lighthouse in the grass;
bare burr oak, stripped winter branches like the skeleton
            of a great brain; the stinging nettle that blistered
your hands when you battled the weeds rimming the
            driveway. When I say
      I miss the prairies,
  what I mean is
I miss you everywhere.
            The entire state bears the soft wet stain
        of your body, the oil of your face pressed

      into the earth like a flag. I have seen just under your skin
    so many times: gathering aronia berries in the
forest: the buckthorn catching your
legs
    tearing the flesh like cheap cloth; fishing knee-
deep
      in the big lake: the zebra mussels
          slicing your feet, blood
            scenting the silty water.
        All the avoidable bike wrecks, trying to
ride
off the path, farther into the wild's messy hold—your feet
tangling   in the mess
        of greased chain, your palms tight with scab

                        and gravel. You were never meant to
leave. The land has staked
            its claim and I was wrong to misjudge its
hold.   Afternoons you spent throwing
                    your long   thin   body
    at the white oak, angled differently each time, reaching
                                again and again
        and again for the lowest branch, until, finally, you
            grabbed it—too tired to pull yourself up, you dangled
            like an oversized child, exhausted and
        victorious; you held on longer than I thought possible.
            When you dropped, the oak's rough bark kept
            some of your hands. You bandaged
the wounds and forgot what you lost.   Bark grew
over
        the bits of flesh you left behind   as the earth reclaims
                everything we lose.   I could have saved
myself   years of want if only I had known, then
        what I would never get back; the slivers of you beneath
bark
                            the cattail seeds that took
                                to the wind.

The Good Stuff

I sip the amber liquid two knuckles high in the short glass, no ice,
though there should be ice, the heat of my hand doing it no
favors. I have drunk a whole finger's worth
of the stuff. I am trying to understand my father's love

for bourbon, how he cradles it for a moment
beneath his tongue before swallowing. Once, he presented me with a
careful pour from his favorite bottle, aged
for most of my life in white oak barrels, burnt black

on the inside to fill the liquor with smoke. The only
proper way. But he didn't say this, just handed me the glass—
so I downed it, threw it back like a shot of tequila.
How could I have known? It all tastes like the end

of a fire. He was horrified, clearly wished he could take it back,
give this precious drink to someone who knew how to enjoy it. I
am sorry for all the times we have missed
each other like this. I am always swallowing what is sweet

and easy. I imagine the ways I could make it
better: salty rim, big dose of maple syrup, calling him
more often, a pour into pecan pie, finally seeing
he has given me the best of everything. I number my sips,

adjoining them to all the cruel things I've said, the bitterness
he never deserved. I am trying. I am trying to savor the notes of oak
and molasses, to learn how corn, yeast, and time yield this rich gold.

Invitation

> *God sends meat and the devil sends cooks.*
> *—Proverb*

No, you don't need to bring anything—I already
have several shades of wine, a white serving plate
heaped with pastries. All day with my face in front
of the oven, above the stove. My wrists freckled
          with oil. I have stretched and risen
the dough, brushed it with beaten egg. It bloomed
gold and round in the heat. No, no, you sit. I'll fill
the glasses. The next course pairs perfectly
with a vieux carré (a recipe I learned this morning
          after googling *classiest cocktail,* then
how to pronounce vieux carré). It's not that I want
to play pretentious—I just want you a little bit
in debt. I want these kindnesses to weigh one side
of the ledger, to pile at the foot of the stairs. I want
          only a small gnawing of guilt
for all I have fed you. Of course, there's dessert.
Poached pear galettes, rosemary sugar. A small
mountain of macarons with their neatly crinkled
feet. Please, take some home with you. When you come
down to your own kitchen late tonight, you'll eat
          a pastry, and think, again, of me.

Jesus in the Foothills

My obaasan asked to stop at an old stone church
as we passed, tucked beside a winding highway
in the Rocky Mountain foothills,

its thick hexagonal spires painting themselves on a back-
drop of early summer mountains: snow powdered and humming.
Three generations of women climbed out of the small silver

sedan—obaasan, mother, daughter—the full burden
of each title bound to the ways we love
each other. We walked around the base, the church

emerging like an impossible coincidence from the pile
of stones beneath it. I was enthralled with the mountain's rocky
skyline, row after row of craggy teeth, each pine

growing from cracked boulders and loamy soil, roots
extending twice as far into inhospitable earth. My obaasan
stayed by the church, her palms against the rock,

cool and smooth from wind and water, fingers gentle
against the stained-glass windows, their bumpy
imperfections. She tugged the huge wooden doors—

they were locked. A blessing. It would have been too much
to enter, the dusky room with all its dark
wood, the fine dust of guilt settling into our clothes.

My obaasan, the only one with a small candle of faith
still wind-sheltered in her chest, stood on the steps
and looked into the sun. She chirped   *Jesus*

and we followed her eyes, stared like children
into the light: tucked into an outcropping above the church
was a statue of him, ice melting into his shoulders, a chickadee

preening on his open hand. She insisted on photos: first the statue
alone, then, camera balanced on the steps, the three of us
gathered dutifully at his feet. In the photo, both my mom and I

look at her, the start of little smiles flicker across
our faces like sunlight through water. My obaasan is caught
in profile, gaze turned upward toward him, a smile so wide

it swallows her eyes. The chickadee had leapt from his hand,
frozen in the weightless moment just before flight.

At the Cemetery

Today: spring in full force. Lark song overlays the low hum
of interstate traffic, this town's wasted heart. Cottonwood blooms

without leaves. Hedge apples flower, tendril petals foreshadowing
the sour fruit. The earth is roiling with insects: field crickets leaping wildly,

battering my legs with their brittle bodies as my Obaasan and I walk
the neat rows. How could anyone stay dead on a day like this? First,

we lay flowers atop Sekiko and Yoshi, her old friends. Purple hyacinths
with their clean rain scent, fringe petaled carnations spicy as sliced chilis.

Then, we search for her babies' headstones, my two almost mothers.
I trail behind her, reading names silently until it has been too long walking

and I realize she is directionless, unable to find what she once held inside her.
This moment: another cruel loss. She doubles back on herself again thinking

she has remembered, touching the top of each stone as if asking a question.
At the end of the row, she finds instead someone else's sorrow. Eventually,

she stops below a flaking sycamore. I pause ten steps behind. A cricket crashes
into my calf. Obaasan rests her hand on the tree's rough bark. She lifts her chin

and cocks her head as if listening for the small sound of a child.

Obed Wild and Scenic River

My body was rich
with evidence of use:
    welts wide and firm as dollar coins,
    toes rubbed raw, forearms splintered

by split wood, some unknown
rash scattering my back
    like rain. Camping alone, I was solitary
    prey, easy quarry for the clouds of river-bred

bugs. I called it negligence:
the DEET unopened in the car,
    citronella and peppermint oil sprayed lazily
    onto my hat. The needle-nosed insects

flecking the exposed parts
of my limbs. But I came for this:
    dissolution of the skin's soft boundary, loss
    of barrier between the world and whatever

I hold. I wanted to surrender
to something, to escape
    the body's rigid container, briefly,
    and be borderless in the wild dark—

drops of my blood suspended by glassy wings,
glittering their bug mouths, beads like tiny

        pomegranate seeds as they
        buzzed away to find

another bare landscape
of flesh, where they'd bite and leave
        a crimson mark of me,
        the stain of a kiss.

Entering the Anza Borrego

Eventually we round the last turn, though we don't know it is the last
until after we're through—and we see it, finally: the great desert
like a flood plain below, spreading its creased palm as far as we can bear
imagining. From here, nothing has edges. Victorious clumps of green bleed
into sand, into heaps of boulders like fallen cairns, into untarnished sky, crisp
and smooth as wind-dried linen. Our noses are already caked with dust,
my grandma and I in her coughing Subaru, taking the slide
down the mountain that spills us onto the dirt choked road, leading us first
into Borrego Springs, then out. On the other side, the smell of citrus
is overwhelming: rows of orange trees, fruits like fist-sized fires alight
in the branches, leaves glossy wet from sprinklers sunk
into the earth, spouting thin streams of what's become precious.
We could be stuck here, driving through these rows while the world's water
turns to orange flesh, seedless and acidic. The oily rinds piling up against
our shins, bits of pith stuck in our hair. We ask for everything
pulp free, strained clean and silky. The whites of our eyes gone
yellow first, then our teeth and weakened bone, so full of this sick sweet
fruit our blood takes a new hue. Every small smile will reveal a crescent
of orange peel. In the end, we will all drink juice and cut slabs of steak
on the ocean floor. But here, now, Grandma's hand
is out the window, fingers licking the hot wind. *These orange trees sure are
beautiful. No wonder California oranges always taste so good.*

My Brother as Anonymous Bather

—after "Mountain Stream," by John Singer Sargent (1914)

The spring after my brother admitted
he was an addict, we spent a week
at the Laurel River, the rush of snow-
melt to wash clean our winter wants,

our fresh guilt. One morning I discovered him
gone, the rented cabin empty except
for the shadow of panic tailing me
like a loyal dog. I stumbled down

to the river, the high water roaring
loud as a bad engine—and there
he was, crouched like Sargent's
anonymous bather, naked and thrilled

by cold, a streak of flesh in the dark
stones. Too close to the great tumble
of white water, his body
possessed the lithe assurance of a man

comfortable at catastrophe's cusp.
He leaned forward, peering into a pool
cut through by sunlight, a crawdad
picking its way over a heap of pebbles

at the bottom. The pool hollowed
by the river's will alone, the surface

stippled from the spray
churning angrily just feet away.

And my little brother—the water's
reflection scattering his face, misted
tangle of hair holding the sun
in chaotic halo—always leaning closer.

IV

Self-Portrait with Francis in My Ear

—after Evie Shockley

Self-portrait with ice cubes, with October's
first nip, with swollen hips and bone
spurs making forest of a spine. Self-

portrait with dead rabbit in the pool's
filter, with the same water spurted
from cinched lips, with the animal

necropolis just beyond the fence. *Self-portrait
with injured eye.* Self-portrait with Francis
tugging at my wrists like a puppet master's

wraith, with my own eye round and dark
as a plum, with his many hands at my chin,
a bouquet of asters. Self-portrait in the Wake

of My Life. Self-portrait with fighting
dogs, with debts I savor like fur or good
butter, with the golden oysters ringing

the oaks, little mute lanterns. Self-portrait
with *the people dying around me* with
cheeks whirlpooling as though the face

were being pulled down some grim drain
with *I've had nobody else to paint but myself*
with grief's penumbra a bleak halo with the terrible
things I've named in my sweetest voice.

Oregon with Wildfire

"Talk to a firefighter if you think that climate change isn't real."
—*L.A. Mayor Eric Garcetti*

some trees need   the fire
    to exhale   seed, to release   what comes next.

      this is   not that. each tree opening   like a box,
flame fingers' wild unbraiding   of the rough bark, the trunks
    thick   as a hundred wrists

acres gone
    less erased than marked out   a black sharpie wide
    as a state   or   the west
every bit of land capped in sky the color of metal   ready to brand
    yards wetted with the garden hose,

the fire   galloping   over the hills: a band
    of horses—
    how to face that kind of power
insatiable and unable to reason
fire can   jump   a mile   or more

    say: *jump*   like it's a beast
hind legs   corded   thick
    with muscle,   eyes   that render a body   as ash
    the smoke like one   long   rising   wail

or the smoke thick as velvet   a red curtain
    lowering over the cast   bowing deep   and
final

            thin bodies   wavering   in the hot light
         it has been closing night   for years
   the audience   on their feet, clapping
                  and   clapping   and   clapping

At Sun Rock Ranch

In the morning, I watched the rancher
pull the calf from its mother—
      his arm submerged to the shoulder,
      trying to right the knobby creature
unsuccessfully. I knew the moment
I saw the cow—alone in the unbearable
      sun, the strange pendulum of flesh
      swinging below, her bloody time-
keeper—the calf wouldn't make it.
It was the summer I first bled, too,
      and I believed it made me wise. Perhaps
      it did: I found the cow. I roped her neck
and led her home, dark fluid
speckling the gold grass like crumbs
      no one would follow. The day plowed
      further into heat. The barn wavered
as if behind a curtain
of water. The calf emerged
      legs first, a small bundle of brushwood.
      The body slipped out as afterthought
pooled in the straw like a towel used
to clean up some terrible violence.
      The mother turned to lick the dead thing
      clean. The barn walls leaned in like funeral
guests—desperate for closeness and unable
to say anything that would make a difference.

My Obaasan Once Made a Skirt of Cranes

—after Hung Liu's Going Away, Coming Home

and now they appear
                everywhere
   like her echo: in the park's shallow pond, dipping
                needle-beak
deep into the sludgy pool in search of food, the cover
                of a notebook abandoned
in the library, at the Oakland airport, their red crowned heads—
                enamel paint dripping
from eighty delicate bird skulls across the broad swath
                of glass.
Liu says the drips are a   *shedding of gravity—*
                a kind of ascension—
far away, it's beautiful: stilled in perpetual sky
                keeping only what they need
                all line and feather.
Up close, it's horrific: the drips as flesh   sloughing off
                beckoned back earthward
                in this way we share   our end.
In myth, cranes live forever—a symbol of good fortune
                longevity, luck.
This feels now   like a cruel irony.
Dear cranes, tell me how to hold this
                hollow-boned grief.
When late afternoon light cuts through the big window,
                the birds appear
like a mirage on the far wall, ghosts
                cast in sunlight.

In the reflection, details are missing: the thin line
             where the beak parts, dark swirl of the eye—
what is the name
          of an echo's echo?
Each time,
       the sound of her voice grows softer.

The Record

Lately I've been obsessed with making
lists, as though lining things up
one by one might finally provide
meaning. I made a list of what I planned
to pack for a trip home, then, after the fact,
a list of what I actually packed. By recording
these things they become more real. *This
Happened.* Once at the bakery I forgot salt
in a huge batch of pastry dough—such dull
butter. Here is the record. All the old people
I know are obsessed with the news—perhaps
because they are desperate still to be a part
of this world or because they have finally learned
to care for people they do not know. I throw salt
over my shoulder, but the devil has a thousand
eyes. I don't want to be so tight-hearted,
but cannot watch closely a paper fortune teller
with every square reading *disaster*. I hardly use
salt in my cooking these days. In a way it is lucky
if your vices kill you—that you earn your end. Randomness
is neither fair nor unfair. I have moved past the age
at which if my parents died people would say

so tragic. That such a horrible thing
is no longer considered *unfair* is so terribly
unfair. Bits of rice in the salt shaker like strange
larva. Bits of rice in the salt shaker that remind
me, like all rice, of my Obaasan. She calls my brother

her *number one grandson*, my mother her *number
one daughter*. She remembers our roles but not
our names, except, sometimes, she remembers
mine, because it is also hers. At least in her forgetfulness
we have all become number one, first in class,
the best versions of ourselves. Worth my weight
in salt. In kimchi brine. I misunderstood the weather,
wore the wrong shoes. The snow soaked mercilessly
into my socks. My Obaasan leaves on the gas
with no flame but knows every anchor, the rhythm
of every talking head. As a child I once ripped open
a small white packet at a restaurant, thrilled
to be doing something just the right amount
of wrong, then poured the fine grain onto my tongue,
expecting sugar.

In Which I Can Forgive My Obaasan

> *Denial is a psychologically incapacitating state that some mothers experience when faced with the possibility that their children are being sexually abused by their partners.*
> —Christine Adams

Pregnant with my mother, she craved fish heads
severed neat at the gills, pyramids of flesh on ice,
dozens in rows with their noses in the air like soldiers
or dogs. Eyes still cradled in their sockets, wet
marbles in the curl of a fist. Every day the bus
to *Heiwadori* market in the flooded heat, then the weight
of the fish on her waning lap. Back
at the army housing, bones emerged from her lips,
stripped clean. The eyes melted like fat on her tongue.
She could not afford to be a woman who turned
away.
      Now, I keep two coins, a stone, black incense
in my pockets when I am with her. Just in case. I will make
her afterlife loaded, heaven rich. I know, I'm mixing
traditions. Worse things have been done
for love. This, like everything, has become an elegy.
It's not cruel to elegize the living. It is rehearsal
for a worthy grief—we must practice together
while she lives. She will teach me how to lose her.

In Which I Cannot

> *Some mothers maintain their state of denial in the face of the most overt signs of sexual abuse. Clues are often present long before the incest begins.*
> —Christine Adams

       my mother,

                                        flesh

in   a fist.

She   turned
away
      Now, I keep

                     no

traditions.
     This   elegy
of a   grief—we must
    live

Origin

where the ache originates: the pull-able
tooth or the whole jaw—the popping joint
catching on itself, splitting wide to swallow
your latest regret. You are helpless

when it comes to knowing what will kill you.
Sometimes the darkness crackles. Or it is
some dark artery, some vital thing you never
knew beat inside you like bad rain. Walking

the dog, you pass three dead birds
on consecutive blocks, small bodies unmarred
by tooth or claw, white bellies facing a white sky.
There you go again, giving small confessions

to keep the pressure manageable, each truth
like a kettle's thin whistle. Yes—the birds
were dead. They were laid out like gifts,
like warnings. What you didn't say: each one

wore the face of someone you wish
you weren't. Yes—each face was one
of yours. As you passed them, I know
you held your breath, the same as passing

a cemetery. You respect your dead and so
you imitate them, empty lunged. Someday
you will have to breathe. Flattering
death will not spare you. Every time

you think *this* is the end it won't be. Then,
when it is, it just is. You will not pass three
dead birds. They will not be an omen. Now,
fill yourself with air. One day you will wake,

toothless, skin lined with canyons enough
to hold an ocean, and you'll know
I did all this for you.

I watch basketball with B and yell

when my favorite player
dunks—yes, I know enough now
to have a favorite player, can quote
stats and bitch at the refs when
it was a flop not a real foul when
it was all ball I swear when his feet
were set and he took the charge
like a champ when there's no time
for us at half time or time
outs or any time, anymore.
There it is, then. What floats to the surface
like a body in every story. A room
of mirrors, our echo traveling
in every direction. This love is a spectator
sport. Vacant stadium. Who to root for
is all about narrative. I explain our distance
like this—it is dull to win the same way
again and again. Star weary. The crowd craves
an arc. The crowd wants the last guy off the bench
making the cut, wants him hot, slick-necked
and flexing. The crowd wants him sinking
every shot. Wants him turning
from the basket as the clock
goes off, his long arms raised toward
the jumbotron, a view of his face
from every angle saying *look,*
look what I've made of myself.

Relapse with Memory
of the Ramsey Cascades

My brother and I riding the ridge
for miles, his feet sodden, having cracked
the river's meager ice. His brief cry

split the trees like buckshot.
My brother and I in wool socks and graceless
boots, cold seeping like a rash

across our cheeks. My brother
and I finally at the waterfall's base,
our faces braced against a clean sky.

Ice encased the falls—winter, a cruel bride,
behind her frozen veil. Beneath the ice, water
still rushed the rock's thin aisles. My brother

and I on the phone to say he is high
again: again, him sunk to his narrow thighs
in the freezing river, again the current

yanking his ankles, staring animal-eyed
at me while I can do nothing. I cannot even call out
his name—a name is an admission

of distance I cannot bear. My brother:
a barren flagpole. My brother's footprints
filled in. No. My brother and I both coming down

the mountain. My brother and I both
coming down the mountain. My brother leaving
his shadow like a stain in the new snow.

Apologia

I'm sorry for every time I closed the curtains
on the morning sun. I'm sorry for eating the whole jar
of pickles, then burying the empty glass beneath coffee
grounds and eggshells, pretending I'd forgotten to buy
them again. I'm sorry the melon man at the Farmer's Market
looked so much like my grandfather I resented his beautiful
fruit. I'm sorry I hear the siren's long thin wail and am reminded
how close we always are to tragedy—tracing the thin line between disaster
and joy. I'm sorry for the time in the cave when the guide
turned off the lights, just for a moment, to show us true
blindness and I felt my mouth fill with salt, felt a fish
nuzzle my throat, wind whistle through my open skull—
I'm sorry to the child beside me on the tour for not confessing
this panic, not wailing alongside her as we searched
for ourselves in the dark. I'm sorry to my obaasan
for the twenty-four years it took me to learn
how to boil an octopus without overcooking. I'm sorry
to my dogs, who have already forgiven all
my small cruelties. I'm sorry that when I feel a shadow
pass over me—the moment something thin as a wing
blocks out the whole sun—I look for my brother
in the sky. I'm sorry it is only me—sickening
stowaway, dark bird—between myself and the sun.
If this is what finally drives the captive elephants
to their dull madness—the huge beasts stamping their feet
in the red dirt, pacing the long strip of electric fence, swinging
their great heads back and forth in rhythm—I am sorry,
so sorry to every elephant I believed was dancing.

Emergence

> *Every block of stone has a statue inside it*
> *and it is the task of the sculptor to discover it.*
> —Michelangelo

As though the sculptor in charge of crafting
his delicate features suddenly got it right,

the face belonging to him emerging
from the stone a little more with every day

sober. So many years of him wearing
someone else's mouth, its bitter slackness,

and the wrong eyes, light-averse
and flighty, rolling like struck cue balls

in their dark hollows. His cheeks no longer sag
like damp rags from the bones of his face.

And my god, I have never seen a man eat
like this, as though it were the first time

he tasted the berry's sweet bite, the steak's
rich juice filling his mouth like revelation.

When his jaw works the fatty meat, the metrical click
of his mandibles from years of panicked grinding

is what remains of his old self, the creature
of midday darkness that once stalked through

my brother's life. I know he still feels the ghosts
of his old appetites roiling his good blood, pacing

the long hallways lined with doors to relapse.
But now, at least now, he's a man who smiles

with his own mouth, blinks his own eyes, moves
with a body relearning the possibilities

of control—to trust the body's weight against
the insistent pull of great heights, steady

hands to mark the chisel's precise angle.
Day after day the angel in the marble

must carve himself free.

Acknowledgments

Barnstorm: "The Record"

Chestnut Review: "My Little Brother Tells Me He's a Drug Addict"

The Cincinnati Review: "Business Ethics"

Four Way Review: "Self-Portrait as Minotaur"

Frontier Poetry: "Cocke County"

Grist: "Apologia"

Harvard Review: "Francis Bacon on *The Black Triptychs*"

Hayden's Ferry Review: "In Which I Can Forgive My Obaasan," "In Which I Cannot," "Sun Rock Ranch"

Mississippi Review: "Invitation"

The Missouri Review: "Emergence" (Poem of the Week)

New South: "Self Portrait with Francis in My Ear"

Painted Bride Quarterly: "What Will Live"

Palette Poetry: "My Brother as Anonymous Bather"

RHINO Poetry: "Black Holes and Their Feeding Habits"

Southeast Review: "On My Way to Being An Actual"

Split Rock Review: "At the Obed Wild and Scenic River," "Oregon with Wildfire"

Sugar House Review: "Portrait of My Brother with His Habit"

SWWIM: "At the Center for Imaging"

*Trampse*t: "My Mother as Cicada"

"Black Holes and Their Feeding Habits" won the RHINO 2022 Ralph Hamilton Editors' Prize.

About the Author

Kiyoko Reidy is a writer from east Tennessee. She received an undergraduate degree from the University of Wisconsin-Madison and her MFA from Vanderbilt University. Her writing has been published in *Creative Nonfiction, Palette Poetry, Four Way Review,* and elsewhere. *Black Holes and Their Feeding Habits* is her debut full-length collection.

www.ingramcontent.com/pod-product-compliance
Lightning Source LLC
Chambersburg PA
CBHW060535080526
44586CB00012B/745